Fix Your F***ing Credit

And Stop Asking To Use Mine

A DIY Approach to Credit Repair

By: **Oliver Firestone**

Copyright © Oliver Firestone

This book is intended for entertainment purposes only and does not constitute legal advice. While the information provided aims to be accurate and helpful, it should not be relied upon as a substitute for professional legal counsel. Readers are encouraged to consult with a qualified attorney for advice on specific legal matters. The author and publisher disclaim any liability for any actions taken based on the information contained in this book.

- Introduction 6
- Importance of a Credit Score 7
- Understanding Credit Reports 8
- Impact of a Credit Score 9
- Goals of the Book 10
- Chapter 1: Getting Started 11
- Accessing Your Credit Situation 12
- Obtaining Your Credit Reports 13
- Understanding Your Credit Scores 14
- Chapter 2: Disputing Inaccuracies 15
- What Constitutes an Inaccuracy 16
- Sample Dispute Letter 17
- Sample Dispute Letters for Inquiries 18
- Sample Dispute Letters for Public Records 19
- Sample Dispute Letters for Personal Information 21
- Addressing Common Errors 22
- Chapter 3: Strategies for Improving Credit 23
- Paying Down Debt 24
- Negotiating with Creditors 25
- Using Secured Credit Cards 26
- Building a Positive Credit History 27
- Avoid Common Pitfalls 28
- Chapter 4: Dealing With Collections 29
- Understanding Collection Agencies 30
- Negotiating Settlements 31
- Pay for Delete Agreements 32
- Sample Letters for Dealing With Collections 33
- Debt Validation Letter 33
- Settlement Offer Letter 34
- Pay for Delete Letter 35
- Chapter 5: Rebuilding Credit 36
- Secured Vs Unsecured Credit 37
- Applying for New Credit 38
- Improving Credit Utilization 39
- Using Credit Builder Loans 40
- Monitoring Progress 41
- Chapter 6: Legal Rights and Resources 42
- Fair Credit Reporting Act (FCRA) 43
- Fair Debt Collection Practices Act (FDCPA) 44
- Consumer Financial Protection Bureau (CFPB) 45

Federal Trade Commission (FTC)	46
Sample Letters for Legal Remedies	47
FCRA Dispute Letter	47
FDCPA Cease and Desist Letter	48
Chapter 7: Advanced Techniques	49
Goodwill Letters	50
Paying for Deletion	52
Rapid Resource	54
Authorized User Strategy	55
Disputing Certified Mail	56
Chapter 8: Long-Term Maintenance	58
Importance of Regular Monitoring	59
Avoiding Credit Repair Scams	60
Staying Financially Responsible	61
Future Planning	62
Chapter 9: Case Studies and Success Stories	63
Real Life Examples of Credit Repair	64
Lessons Learned	66
Inspiration for Readers	67
Chapter 10: Additional Resources	68
Contact Information for Credit Bureaus	69
Contact Information for Consumer Agencies	70
Recommended Books and Websites	71
Glossary of Terms	72
Conclusion	74
Recap of Points	75
Encouragement for the Future	76
Other Books By This Publisher	77
About This Author	78
Review This Book	79

Description

This is written for people who need help repairing their credit. It's for those who are tired of paying higher interest on the credit they do have and those who have to get someone to co-sign for them before they can purchase the things they need.

If you're looking for a sugar-coated book you're in the wrong place. We're not here to spare your feelings. We're here to get you to a place where you will never have to bother your family or friends again for a loan or help to obtain one.

People with bad credit pay more than people with good credit for most everything. They pay higher insurance premiums, and higher interest rates and are sometimes turned down for the job they want when a credit check is required.

It's not fair to the people who did a good job with their credit and has lived within their means when you come knocking on their doors when you need something new. I'm sure your friends and family will appreciate your effort to clean up your own act and you might find that you can now have a better quality of friends when they're not always needing to avoid your phone calls or visits.

We're going to dive in quickly on the credit repair knowledge you'll need to know to make it happen.

> Most people don't find themselves in this way overnight, and you will most likely not get yourself out of it overnight, but with our guidance, you will hopefully find you can get back to a good credit report within a few months.

This outline provides a comprehensive guide to repairing credit, covering everything from disputing inaccuracies to rebuilding credit and long-term maintenance. By including sample letters, legal resources, and case studies, readers will have the tools and knowledge to fix their failing credit and achieve financial stability.

Introduction

In today's world, your credit score plays a crucial role in your financial well-being. Whether you're applying for a loan, renting an apartment, or even securing a job, your credit score often determines your eligibility and the terms you're offered. Unfortunately, many people find themselves struggling with poor credit due to various reasons, from missed payments to identity theft. The good news is that no matter how dire your credit situation may seem, there are steps you can take to repair and improve it.

Importance of a Credit Score

Your credit score is a numerical representation of your creditworthiness, calculated based on your credit history. It ranges from 300 to 850, with higher scores indicating lower credit risk. Lenders, landlords, and even potential employers use this score to assess the risk of doing business with you. A high credit score can lead to lower interest rates on loans, higher credit limits, and better opportunities overall. On the other hand, a low credit score can result in higher interest rates, limited access to credit, and even denials for loans or housing.

Understanding how your credit score is calculated is essential for improving it. The factors that influence your score include your payment history, credit utilization ratio, length of credit history, types of credit used, and new credit inquiries. By knowing what affects your score, you can take targeted actions to improve it.

Understanding Credit Reports

Your credit report is a detailed record of your credit history, compiled by credit bureaus such as Experian, Equifax, and TransUnion. It contains information about your credit accounts, payment history, outstanding balances, and any negative items such as late payments, collections, or bankruptcies. Reviewing your credit report regularly is crucial for spotting errors and identifying areas for improvement.

Credit reports can be obtained for free once a year from each of the major credit bureaus through AnnualCreditReport.com. Additionally, many credit monitoring services offer access to your credit report and score on a regular basis. When reviewing your report, pay attention to any inaccuracies or discrepancies, as these can negatively impact your credit score.

Impact of a Credit Score

The consequences of poor credit can be far-reaching and affect various aspects of your life. Financially, it can lead to higher interest rates on loans and credit cards, making it more expensive to borrow money. It can also result in lower credit limits and difficulty obtaining new credit. Poor credit can also affect your ability to rent an apartment, as landlords often run credit checks on prospective tenants. Some employers even check credit reports as part of the hiring process, potentially impacting your job prospects.

Beyond the financial implications, poor credit can also take a toll on your mental and emotional well-being. Constantly worrying about debt, struggling to make ends meet, and feeling hopeless about your financial future can lead to stress, anxiety, and depression.

Goals of the Book

The primary goal of this book is to empower you to take control of your credit and improve your financial situation. Whether you're dealing with past mistakes, inaccuracies on your credit report, or unforeseen financial hardships, there are steps you can take to repair your credit and move forward.

Throughout the following chapters, we will provide you with practical strategies, expert advice, and actionable tips for repairing your credit. From disputing inaccuracies to negotiating with creditors, rebuilding credit, and maintaining long-term financial health, this book covers everything you need to know to fix your failing credit. Our aim is to equip you with the knowledge and tools necessary to achieve a better credit score and a brighter financial future.

Chapter 1: Getting Started

Before diving into the process of repairing your credit, it's essential to understand where you currently stand. This chapter will guide you through the initial steps of assessing your credit situation, obtaining your credit reports, and understanding credit scores.

Accessing Your Credit Situation

Assessing your credit situation involves taking a close look at your financial history, current debts, and credit habits. This step is crucial as it provides insight into the factors influencing your credit score and helps identify areas for improvement.

Start by gathering all relevant financial documents, including credit card statements, loan statements, and any other debt obligations. Create a comprehensive list of all your creditors, including their contact information and outstanding balances. This will give you a clear overview of your debts and who you owe money to.

Next, review your payment history for each account. Late payments, missed payments, and accounts in collections can significantly impact your credit score. Make note of any negative items on your credit report, such as late payments, charge-offs, or accounts in collections.

Once you have a complete picture of your debts and payment history, calculate your credit utilization ratio. This ratio represents the amount of credit you're using compared to the total credit available to you. Ideally, you want to keep your credit utilization below 30% to maintain a good credit score. If your utilization ratio is high, consider paying down your balances to improve your score.

Assessing your credit situation also involves identifying any errors or inaccuracies on your credit report. Common errors include accounts that don't belong to you, incorrect account statuses, and outdated information. Disputing these errors is essential for ensuring that your credit report accurately reflects your financial history.

Obtaining Your Credit Reports

Obtaining your credit reports is the next crucial step in the credit repair process. Your credit reports contain detailed information about your credit accounts, payment history, and other factors that contribute to your credit score.

You are entitled to a free copy of your credit report from each of the three major credit bureaus—Experian, Equifax, and TransUnion—every 12 months. The official website to request these reports is AnnualCreditReport.com. Alternatively, you can contact each credit bureau individually to request your report.

When requesting your credit reports, be prepared to provide personal information such as your name, address, Social Security number, and date of birth. You may also need to answer security questions to verify your identity.

Once you receive your credit reports, review them carefully for accuracy. Pay close attention to the following:

1. Personal Information: Ensure that your name, address, and other identifying information are correct.
2. Account Information: Review each account listed on your report to verify that it belongs to you and that the information is accurate. Check the account status, balance, payment history, and any negative items associated with each account.
3. Inquiries: Take note of any recent inquiries into your credit report. Too many inquiries within a short period can negatively impact your credit score.
4. Public Records: Check for any public records such as bankruptcies, judgments, or liens. These items can have a significant impact on your credit score.
5. Errors or Inaccuracies: If you spot any errors or inaccuracies on your credit report, such as accounts you don't recognize or incorrect payment statuses, it's essential to dispute them with the credit bureaus.

Understanding Your Credit Scores

Understanding how credit scores work is fundamental to improving your credit. Your credit score is a numerical representation of your creditworthiness, based on information in your credit report. Several factors contribute to your credit score, each carrying a different weight:

1. Payment History (35%): Your payment history is the most crucial factor influencing your credit score. It indicates whether you've paid your bills on time and accounts for 35% of your score.
2. Credit Utilization (30%): Credit utilization refers to the amount of credit you're using compared to your total available credit. Keeping your credit utilization below 30% is ideal, as it accounts for 30% of your credit score.
3. Length of Credit History (15%): The length of your credit history measures how long you've had credit accounts open. A longer credit history generally results in a higher credit score.
4. Types of Credit Used (10%): Lenders like to see a mix of different types of credit, such as credit cards, installment loans, and mortgages. This factor accounts for 10% of your credit score.
5. New Credit (10%): Opening several new credit accounts in a short period can negatively impact your credit score. New credit inquiries and accounts make up 10% of your score.

Understanding these factors allows you to take targeted actions to improve your credit score. For example, focusing on paying bills on time, reducing credit card balances, and maintaining a diverse credit portfolio can help boost your score over time.

In the following chapters, we'll delve deeper into strategies for disputing inaccuracies, negotiating with creditors, and rebuilding your credit. By understanding your credit situation, obtaining your credit reports, and comprehending credit scores, you'll be well-equipped to embark on your credit repair journey and achieve financial stability.

Chapter 2: Disputing Inaccuracies

One of the most critical steps in repairing your credit is disputing inaccuracies on your credit report. Inaccurate information can have a significant impact on your credit score, potentially leading to higher interest rates, denied credit applications, and other financial setbacks. This chapter will guide you through the process of identifying and disputing inaccuracies on your credit report, providing sample dispute letters and addressing common errors.

What Constitutes an Inaccuracy

Before disputing any information on your credit report, it's essential to understand what constitutes an inaccuracy. Inaccurate information includes anything that is incorrect, outdated, or does not belong to you. Common inaccuracies on credit reports may include:

1. Incorrect Account Information: This includes accounts that don't belong to you, accounts with incorrect balances, and accounts with inaccurate payment histories.
2. Fraudulent Accounts: If you've been a victim of identity theft, you may find accounts on your credit report that you didn't open or authorize.
3. Outdated Information: Negative items such as late payments, collections, or bankruptcies should be removed from your credit report after a certain period, typically seven to ten years, depending on the type of item.
4. Incorrect Personal Information: Your credit report should accurately reflect your name, address, Social Security number, and other identifying information. Incorrect personal information can indicate identity theft or reporting errors.
5. Duplicate Entries: Sometimes, the same account may appear multiple times on your credit report, artificially inflating your debt or negative items.

Identifying inaccuracies is the first step in the dispute process. Once you've identified inaccurate information on your credit report, you can begin the process of disputing it with the credit bureaus.

Sample Dispute Letter

When disputing inaccurate account information on your credit report, it's crucial to provide detailed information and evidence to support your claim. Below is a sample dispute letter template that you can use to dispute account inaccuracies:

[Your Name]
[Your Address]
[City, State, Zip Code]

[Date]

[Credit Bureau Name]
[Address]

[City, State, Zip Code]

Dear Sir/Madam,

I am writing to dispute the following account(s) listed on my credit report. I believe that the information reported is inaccurate and should be investigated and corrected.

Account Information:

Creditor Name: [Name of Creditor]
Account Number: [Account Number]
Date Opened: [Date Opened]
Current Balance: [Current Balance]

Status: [Status]

Explanation of Dispute: [Provide a detailed explanation of why you believe the information is inaccurate. Include any supporting documentation, such as payment records or correspondence with the creditor.]

I request that you investigate this matter and correct the inaccurate information as soon as possible. Please provide me with written confirmation of the actions taken to resolve this dispute.

Sincerely,

[Your Name]

Sample Dispute Letters for Inquiries

Inquiries on your credit report occur when a lender or creditor checks your credit as part of the application process. Too many inquiries within a short period can negatively impact your credit score. If you believe that an inquiry on your credit report is inaccurate or unauthorized, you can dispute it with the credit bureaus. Here's a sample dispute letter template for inquiries:

[Your Name]
[Your Address]
[City, State, Zip Code]

[Date]

[Credit Bureau Name]
[Address]

[City, State, Zip Code]

Dear Sir/Madam,

I am writing to dispute the following inquiry(s) listed on my credit report. I believe that the inquiry(s) is inaccurate or unauthorized and should be investigated and removed.

Inquiry Information:

Creditor Name: [Name of Creditor]
Date of Inquiry: [Date of Inquiry]

Type of Inquiry: [Hard or Soft Inquiry]

Explanation of Dispute: [Provide a detailed explanation of why you believe the inquiry is inaccurate or unauthorized. Include any supporting documentation, such as proof that you did not apply for credit with the creditor.]

I request that you investigate this matter and remove the inquiry(s) from my credit report as soon as possible. Please provide me with written confirmation of the actions taken to resolve this dispute.

Sincerely,

[Your Name]

Sample Dispute Letters for Public Records

Public records such as bankruptcies, judgments, and tax liens can have a significant negative impact on your credit score. If you believe that a public record on your credit report is inaccurate or outdated, you can dispute it with the credit bureaus. Here's a sample dispute letter template for public records:

[Your Name]
[Your Address]
[City, State, Zip Code]

[Date]

[Credit Bureau Name]
[Address]

[City, State, Zip Code]

Dear Sir/Madam,

I am writing to dispute the following public record(s) listed on my credit report. I believe that the information reported is inaccurate or outdated and should be investigated and corrected.

Public Record Information:

Type of Public Record: [Bankruptcy, Judgment, Tax Lien, etc.]
Filing Date: [Filing Date]
Amount: [Amount]
Court Name: [Court Name]

Case Number: [Case Number]

Explanation of Dispute: [Provide a detailed explanation of why you believe the public record is inaccurate or outdated. Include any supporting documentation, such as discharge papers or court documents.]

I request that you investigate this matter and correct the inaccurate or outdated information as soon as possible. Please provide me with written confirmation of the actions taken to resolve this dispute.

Sincerely,

[Your Name]

Sample Disputes Letters for Personal Information

Personal information such as your name, address, and Social Security number should be accurately reflected on your credit report. If you believe that personal information on your credit report is incorrect, you can dispute it with the credit bureaus. Here's a sample dispute letter template for personal information:

[Your Name]
[Your Address]
[City, State, Zip Code]

[Date]

[Credit Bureau Name]
[Address]

[City, State, Zip Code]

Dear Sir/Madam,

I am writing to dispute the following personal information listed on my credit report. I believe that the information reported is inaccurate and should be investigated and corrected.

Personal Information:

Name: [Incorrect Name]
Address: [Incorrect Address]

Social Security Number: [Incorrect SSN]

Explanation of Dispute: [Provide a detailed explanation of why you believe the personal information is inaccurate. Include any supporting documentation, such as a copy of your driver's license or Social Security card.]

I request that you investigate this matter and correct the inaccurate information as soon as possible. Please provide me with written confirmation of the actions taken to resolve this dispute.

Sincerely,

[Your Name]

Addressing Common Errors

While disputing inaccuracies on your credit report, you may encounter common errors that can delay the process or result in the dispute being rejected. It's essential to address these errors proactively to ensure that your dispute is resolved successfully. Some common errors to watch out for include:

1. Incomplete Information: Ensure that all required fields in your dispute letter are filled out completely and accurately. Missing or incomplete information can result in delays or rejection of your dispute.
2. Lack of Documentation: Include any relevant documentation to support your dispute, such as copies of bills, payment records, or correspondence with creditors. Providing evidence strengthens your case and increases the likelihood of a successful resolution.
3. Failure to Follow Up: After submitting your dispute, follow up regularly with the credit bureaus to check the status of your dispute and ensure that it is being processed. Failure to follow up can result in disputes being overlooked or forgotten.
4. Disputing Legitimate Information: Only dispute information that is genuinely inaccurate or outdated. Disputing legitimate information can result in the dispute being rejected and damage your credibility with the credit bureaus.
5. Not Sending Disputes via Certified Mail: Send your dispute letters via certified mail with return receipt requested to ensure that they are received and processed by the credit bureaus. This provides proof of delivery and gives you a record of when the dispute was received.

By addressing these common errors and using the sample dispute letter templates provided, you can effectively dispute inaccuracies on your credit report and take the first step towards repairing your credit. In the following chapters, we'll explore strategies for negotiating with creditors, rebuilding credit, and maintaining long-term financial health.

Chapter 3: Strategies for Improving Credit

Improving your credit score is a journey that requires commitment, patience, and strategic planning. In this chapter, we'll explore various strategies you can implement to boost your credit score and achieve financial stability.

Paying Down Debt

One of the most effective ways to improve your credit score is by paying down your existing debt. High levels of debt can negatively impact your credit utilization ratio, which accounts for 30% of your credit score. Here are some strategies for paying down debt:

1. Create a Budget: Start by creating a realistic budget that outlines your income, expenses, and debt obligations. Allocate a portion of your income towards paying down debt each month.
2. Prioritize High-Interest Debt: Focus on paying off high-interest debt first, such as credit card balances. Paying off high-interest debt saves you money on interest and improves your credit utilization ratio.
3. Use the Debt Snowball or Avalanche Method: The debt snowball method involves paying off the smallest debts first, while the debt avalanche method focuses on paying off the debts with the highest interest rates first. Choose the method that works best for you and stick to it.
4. Increase Your Income: Consider finding ways to increase your income, such as taking on a part-time job, freelancing, or selling items you no longer need. Use the extra income to accelerate debt repayment.
5. Negotiate with Creditors: Contact your creditors to negotiate lower interest rates or payment plans that fit your budget. Many creditors are willing to work with you if you're proactive about addressing your debt.
6. Avoid Taking on New Debt: While you're focused on paying down existing debt, avoid taking on new debt whenever possible. This includes avoiding unnecessary purchases and using credit cards sparingly.

By making a concerted effort to pay down debt, you'll not only improve your credit score but also move closer to financial freedom.

Negotiating with Creditors

If you're struggling to keep up with your debt payments, don't hesitate to reach out to your creditors to discuss your situation. Many creditors are willing to work with you to find a solution that benefits both parties. Here are some tips for negotiating with creditors:

1. Be Proactive: Contact your creditors as soon as you realize you're having difficulty making payments. Ignoring the problem will only make it worse.
2. Explain Your Situation: Be honest and transparent about your financial situation. Explain any extenuating circumstances that have led to your inability to pay, such as job loss, medical expenses, or divorce.
3. Propose a Payment Plan: Offer to make reduced payments or negotiate a payment plan that fits your budget. Be prepared to provide evidence of your income and expenses to support your proposed plan.
4. Ask for Lower Interest Rates: Request a lower interest rate, especially if you have a history of on-time payments. Lower interest rates can reduce the total amount you owe and make it easier to pay off your debt.
5. Get Agreements in Writing: Once you've reached a resolution with your creditor, make sure to get the agreement in writing. This protects you from any misunderstandings or changes to the terms later on.
6. Consider Debt Settlement: If you're unable to pay the full amount owed, you may be able to negotiate a settlement with your creditor. Debt settlement involves paying a lump sum that is less than the total amount owed in exchange for the creditor forgiving the remaining balance.

Negotiating with creditors can be intimidating, but it's often a necessary step towards resolving your debt and improving your credit score.

Using Secured Credit Cards

Secured credit cards are an excellent tool for rebuilding credit, especially if you have a limited credit history or poor credit. Unlike traditional credit cards, secured cards require a security deposit, which serves as collateral for the credit limit. Here's how to use secured credit cards to improve your credit:

1. Choose the Right Card: Look for a secured credit card with low fees and a reasonable interest rate. Compare offers from different banks and credit card issuers to find the best option for your needs.
2. Make Timely Payments: Use your secured credit card responsibly by making timely payments each month. Payment history accounts for 35% of your credit score, so paying your bills on time is crucial for improving your credit.
3. Keep Balances Low: Keep your credit utilization ratio low by only using a small portion of your available credit. Ideally, you should keep your balances below 30% of your credit limit to avoid negatively impacting your credit score.
4. Monitor Your Credit Score: Keep track of your credit score and credit report regularly to monitor your progress. Many secured credit card issuers offer free credit score monitoring as a perk for cardholders.
5. Upgrade to an Unsecured Card: After using your secured credit card responsibly for a period of time, you may be eligible to upgrade to an unsecured credit card. This typically involves returning your security deposit and transitioning to a traditional credit card with a higher credit limit.

Secured credit cards can be a valuable tool for building or rebuilding credit, but it's essential to use them responsibly to see the desired results.

Building a Positive Credit History

Building a positive credit history is essential for improving your credit score and demonstrating your creditworthiness to lenders. Here are some strategies for building positive credit history:

1. Pay Bills on Time: Your payment history is the most crucial factor in your credit score, so make sure to pay all your bills on time, every time.
2. Use Credit Responsibly: Use credit cards and loans responsibly, only borrowing what you can afford to repay. Avoid maxing out your credit cards and keep balances low to maintain a healthy credit utilization ratio.
3. Diversify Your Credit: Having a mix of different types of credit, such as credit cards, installment loans, and mortgages, can improve your credit score. However, only take on new credit accounts when necessary and avoid applying for multiple accounts at once.
4. Keep Old Accounts Open: The length of your credit history matters, so avoid closing old credit accounts, even if you're not using them regularly. Keeping old accounts open demonstrates a longer credit history and can positively impact your score.
5. Become an Authorized User: If you have a trusted friend or family member with good credit, ask them to add you as an authorized user on their credit card account. Being an authorized user allows you to benefit from their positive credit history.

Building positive credit history takes time and consistent effort, but it's an essential step towards improving your credit score and achieving your financial goals.

Avoid Common Pitfalls

While working to improve your credit, it's essential to avoid common pitfalls that can hinder your progress. Here are some common mistakes to avoid:

1. Ignoring Your Credit Report: Regularly monitor your credit report for inaccuracies and signs of identity theft. Ignoring your credit report can result in missed opportunities to correct errors and improve your credit score.
2. Closing Old Accounts: Closing old credit accounts can shorten your credit history and negatively impact your credit score. Keep old accounts open, even if you're not using them regularly.
3. Maxing Out Credit Cards: Keeping high balances on your credit cards can increase your credit utilization ratio and negatively impact your credit score. Aim to keep balances below 30% of your credit limit.
4. Applying for Too Much New Credit: Each time you apply for new credit, a hard inquiry is added to your credit report, which can temporarily lower your credit score. Avoid applying for multiple new accounts at once.
5. Ignoring Your Debt: Ignoring your debt won't make it go away. Address your debt head-on by creating a repayment plan and negotiating with creditors to find a solution that works for you.

By avoiding these common pitfalls and implementing the strategies outlined in this chapter, you'll be well on your way to improving your credit score and achieving financial success. In the following chapters, we'll explore advanced techniques for credit repair and long-term maintenance strategies.

Chapter 4: Dealing With Collections

Dealing with collections can be one of the most challenging aspects of credit repair, but it's essential for improving your credit score and financial health. In this chapter, we'll delve into the intricacies of dealing with collection agencies, negotiating settlements, pay-for-delete agreements, and provide sample letters to aid you in the process.

Understanding Collection Agencies

Collection agencies are third-party companies hired by creditors to recover unpaid debts. These agencies purchase debts from original creditors or work on a contingency basis, earning a percentage of the amount they collect. When a debt is sent to collections, it typically means the original creditor has given up trying to collect the debt and has transferred it to a collection agency.

Collection agencies employ various tactics to collect on debts, including phone calls, letters, and reporting the debt to credit bureaus. It's crucial to understand your rights when dealing with collection agencies. The Fair Debt Collection Practices Act (FDCPA) outlines rules that collection agencies must follow when attempting to collect a debt. These rules include:

- Contacting debtors at reasonable times.
- Providing validation of the debt upon request.
- Ceasing communication if the debtor requests it in writing.
- Not using abusive or threatening language.

Knowing your rights can help you navigate interactions with collection agencies and protect yourself from harassment or unfair practices.

Negotiating Settlements

When dealing with collections, one option is to negotiate a settlement with the collection agency. A settlement involves agreeing to pay a portion of the debt in exchange for the collection agency closing the account and ceasing collection efforts. Here are some tips for negotiating settlements:

1. Start with a Low Offer: Begin negotiations by offering to pay a percentage of the total amount owed, typically starting at around 30% to 50% of the original debt.
2. Get the Agreement in Writing: Once you've reached a settlement agreement with the collection agency, make sure to get the terms in writing before making any payments. This protects you from any changes to the agreement later on.
3. Negotiate Removal of Negative Information: Try to negotiate with the collection agency to have the account removed from your credit report entirely, rather than just marked as "settled." This can significantly improve your credit score.
4. Consider Lump Sum vs. Payment Plan: Collection agencies may be more willing to negotiate a lower settlement amount if you can pay it in a lump sum. However, if you can't afford a lump sum payment, you may be able to negotiate a payment plan instead.
5. Be Persistent: Don't be afraid to negotiate and advocate for yourself. Collection agencies are often willing to work with you to reach a mutually beneficial agreement.

Negotiating settlements with collection agencies can be a daunting process, but it's often worth it to resolve the debt and improve your credit score.

Pay for Delete Agreements

A pay-for-delete agreement is a negotiation tactic where you offer to pay the debt in exchange for the collection agency removing the account from your credit report entirely. While not all collection agencies will agree to a pay-for-delete, it's worth trying, especially if the debt is significantly impacting your credit score. Here's how to negotiate a pay-for-delete agreement:

1. Initiate Contact: Reach out to the collection agency either by phone or in writing to propose a pay-for-delete agreement.
2. Offer to Pay the Debt: Explain that you're willing to pay the debt in full or settle for a lower amount in exchange for the account being removed from your credit report.
3. Get the Agreement in Writing: If the collection agency agrees to a pay-for-delete, make sure to get the terms of the agreement in writing before making any payments.
4. Follow Up: After making the payment, follow up with the collection agency to ensure that they've upheld their end of the agreement and removed the account from your credit report.

While pay-for-delete agreements aren't guaranteed, they can be a powerful tool for improving your credit score and removing negative information from your credit report.

Sample Letters for Dealing With Collections

When communicating with collection agencies, it's essential to do so in writing to have a record of your interactions. Below are sample letters for various situations when dealing with collections:

Debt Validation Letter

[Your Name]
[Your Address]
[City, State, Zip Code]

[Date]

[Collection Agency Name]
[Address]

[City, State, Zip Code]

Subject: Debt Validation Request

Dear Sir/Madam,

I am writing to request validation of the debt you are attempting to collect on. I received a collection notice from your agency dated [Date], referencing an alleged debt in the amount of [Amount].

According to the Fair Debt Collection Practices Act (FDCPA), I have the right to request validation of the debt. Please provide me with the following information:

1. Verification that the debt is valid and legally owed by me.
2. Documentation showing the original creditor and the nature of the debt.
3. Proof that you are licensed to collect debts in my state.

If you cannot provide validation of the debt, you are required to cease collection efforts immediately and remove the account from my credit report.

Sincerely,

[Your Name]

Settlement Offer Letter

[Your Name]
[Your Address]
[City, State, Zip Code]

[Date]

[Collection Agency Name]
[Address]

[City, State, Zip Code]

Subject: Settlement Offer for Account [Account Number]

Dear Sir/Madam,

I am writing to propose a settlement offer for the debt referenced in your recent communication dated [Date]. I acknowledge the debt and am willing to resolve it in exchange for the following terms:

- I agree to pay [Settlement Amount] in full satisfaction of the debt.
- Upon receipt of the settlement payment, you agree to mark the account as "paid" and remove it from all three major credit bureaus' records.

Please confirm your acceptance of these terms in writing, and I will arrange for payment accordingly.

Sincerely,

[Your Name]

Pay for Delete Letter

[Your Name]
[Your Address]
[City, State, Zip Code]

[Date]

[Collection Agency Name]
[Address]

[City, State, Zip Code]

Subject: Pay-for-Delete Agreement for Account [Account Number]

Dear Sir/Madam,

I am writing to propose a pay-for-delete agreement for the debt referenced in your recent communication dated [Date]. I acknowledge the debt and am willing to pay it in full in exchange for the following terms:

- I agree to pay the full amount of [Debt Amount].
- Upon receipt of the payment, you agree to delete the account from all three major credit bureaus' records.

Please confirm your acceptance of these terms in writing, and I will arrange for payment accordingly.

Sincerely,

[Your Name]

By using these sample letters and strategies for dealing with collections, you can take proactive steps to resolve your debts and improve your credit score. In the next chapters, we'll explore advanced techniques for credit repair and long-term financial stability.

Chapter 5: Rebuilding Credit

Rebuilding your credit is a process that requires patience, discipline, and a strategic approach. In this chapter, we'll explore various methods and techniques you can use to rebuild your credit and achieve financial stability.

Secured Vs Unsecured Credit

Understanding the difference between secured and unsecured credit is essential when rebuilding your credit. Secured credit requires collateral, while unsecured credit does not. Here's how they differ:

1. Secured Credit: Secured credit requires you to provide collateral, such as a cash deposit or asset, to secure the credit line. Secured credit cards and secured loans are common examples of secured credit. With a secured credit card, for example, you'll need to make a cash deposit, which serves as collateral and determines your credit limit.Pros of Secured Credit:
    - Easier to qualify for, even with bad credit.
    - Helps establish or rebuild credit history.
    - Can have lower interest rates compared to unsecured credit for those with poor credit.
2. Cons of Secured Credit:
    - Requires an upfront deposit or collateral.
    - Limited credit limits.
    - May have higher fees and interest rates than unsecured credit for those with poor credit.
3. Unsecured Credit: Unsecured credit does not require collateral and is typically based on your creditworthiness. Credit cards, personal loans, and student loans are common examples of unsecured credit. Lenders assess your credit history, income, and other factors to determine your eligibility and credit limit.Pros of Unsecured Credit:
    - No need for collateral.
    - Higher credit limits compared to secured credit.
    - More flexibility in terms of usage.
4. Cons of Unsecured Credit:
    - Harder to qualify for with bad credit.
    - Higher interest rates and fees for those with poor credit.
    - Defaulting can result in legal action and damage to credit score.

When rebuilding credit, secured credit can be an excellent option to start with, especially if you have a limited credit history or poor credit. As you demonstrate responsible credit behavior, you may qualify for unsecured credit products, which can further help rebuild your credit.

Applying for New Credit

When rebuilding your credit, applying for new credit can be both a helpful tool and a potential risk. Here are some tips to consider when applying for new credit:

1. Research Credit Options: Look for credit products designed for individuals with poor or no credit history. Secured credit cards, starter credit cards, and credit builder loans are good options to explore.
2. Apply Sparingly: Avoid applying for multiple credit cards or loans at once. Each application results in a hard inquiry on your credit report, which can temporarily lower your credit score.
3. Read the Terms Carefully: Before applying for a new credit card or loan, make sure to read the terms and conditions carefully. Pay attention to interest rates, fees, and any penalties for late payments.
4. Focus on Secured Credit: Consider starting with a secured credit card or credit builder loan to establish a positive payment history and rebuild your credit gradually.
5. Pre-Qualify if Possible: Some lenders offer pre-qualification options that allow you to check your eligibility for credit products without impacting your credit score. Take advantage of these options to gauge your chances of approval.

When applying for new credit, it's essential to be selective and strategic. Focus on credit products that will help you rebuild your credit and avoid those that could potentially harm your financial situation.

Improving Credit Utilization

Credit utilization refers to the amount of credit you're using compared to your total available credit. It's a crucial factor in your credit score, accounting for 30% of your FICO score. Here's how to improve your credit utilization:

1. Pay Down Balances: The most effective way to improve your credit utilization is by paying down credit card balances. Aim to keep your credit card balances below 30% of your credit limit.
2. Increase Credit Limits: Another way to improve your credit utilization is by increasing your credit limits. Contact your credit card issuer to request a credit limit increase, but be aware that this may result in a hard inquiry on your credit report.
3. Use Credit Wisely: Use credit cards sparingly and avoid maxing out your credit limits. Keeping balances low demonstrates responsible credit behavior and can positively impact your credit score.
4. Avoid Closing Old Accounts: Closing old credit accounts can reduce your available credit and increase your credit utilization ratio. Keep old accounts open, even if you're not using them regularly.
5. Pay on Time: Make all credit card payments on time to avoid late fees and penalties. Late payments can negatively impact your credit score and credit utilization ratio.

Improving your credit utilization ratio takes time and discipline, but it's a crucial step in rebuilding your credit and improving your credit score.

Using Credit Builder Loans

Credit builder loans are a type of installment loan designed to help individuals build or rebuild credit. Unlike traditional loans, the funds from a credit builder loan are held in a savings account or certificate of deposit (CD) and released to you after you've made all the payments. Here's how credit builder loans work:

1. Apply for the Loan: Apply for a credit builder loan with a bank or credit union that offers this type of product. You'll typically need to provide proof of income and undergo a credit check, but approval is often easier than with traditional loans.
2. Make Payments on Time: Once approved, you'll make monthly payments towards the loan amount. These payments are reported to the credit bureaus, helping to establish a positive payment history.
3. Build Savings: The funds from the loan are held in a savings account or CD until the loan is paid off. This allows you to build savings while simultaneously improving your credit.
4. Receive the Funds: Once you've made all the payments on the loan, the funds are released to you, and you can use them as you wish. Some lenders may also offer a small interest payment as an incentive.

Credit builder loans are a safe and effective way to build credit, especially for those with limited or poor credit history. By making on-time payments, you can establish a positive credit history and improve your credit score over time.

Monitoring Progress

Monitoring your credit progress is essential when rebuilding your credit. Here's how to monitor your progress effectively:

1. Check Your Credit Report Regularly: Monitor your credit report regularly to track changes and identify any errors or inaccuracies. You're entitled to a free copy of your credit report from each of the three major credit bureaus (Equifax, Experian, and TransUnion) every 12 months through AnnualCreditReport.com.
2. Use Credit Monitoring Services: Consider using credit monitoring services that provide real-time alerts and updates on changes to your credit report. Many credit card issuers and financial institutions offer this service for free to their customers.
3. Track Your Credit Score: Keep track of your credit score to monitor your overall credit health. You can access your credit score for free through various online platforms and credit monitoring services.
4. Set Goals: Set specific goals for improving your credit, such as increasing your credit score by a certain number of points or paying off a specific debt. Track your progress towards these goals regularly.
5. Address Issues Promptly: If you identify any errors or inaccuracies on your credit report, take steps to address them promptly. Dispute any inaccuracies with the credit bureaus and follow up to ensure they are corrected.

By monitoring your credit progress regularly, you can stay on track towards rebuilding your credit and achieving your financial goals.

Rebuilding your credit takes time, commitment, and a proactive approach. By understanding the different methods and techniques available, you can take control of your financial future and rebuild your credit effectively. In the following chapters, we'll explore advanced strategies for credit repair and long-term financial success.

Chapter 6: Legal Rights and Resources

Understanding your legal rights as a consumer is crucial when dealing with credit issues. In this chapter, we'll explore key laws that protect consumers' rights, important regulatory agencies, and provide sample letters for legal remedies.

Fair Credit Reporting Act (FCRA)

The Fair Credit Reporting Act (FCRA) is a federal law that regulates the collection, dissemination, and use of consumer credit information. Enacted in 1970, the FCRA aims to promote accuracy, fairness, and privacy of information in consumer credit reports. Here's an overview of key provisions of the FCRA:

1. Access to Credit Reports: Under the FCRA, consumers have the right to obtain a free copy of their credit report from each of the three major credit bureaus (Equifax, Experian, and TransUnion) once every 12 months through AnnualCreditReport.com.
2. Dispute Process: The FCRA provides consumers with the right to dispute inaccurate or incomplete information on their credit reports. Credit bureaus are required to investigate disputes and correct any errors within 30 days.
3. Accuracy of Information: Creditors and credit bureaus are responsible for reporting accurate information to consumer credit reports. If a creditor reports inaccurate information, they must correct it upon notification from the consumer.
4. Identity Theft Protection: The FCRA provides protections for victims of identity theft, including the right to place a fraud alert or credit freeze on their credit report to prevent unauthorized access.
5. Adverse Action Notices: If a creditor takes adverse action, such as denying credit or employment based on information in a credit report, they are required to provide the consumer with a notice explaining the action taken and the consumer's rights under the FCRA.

The FCRA is a powerful tool for consumers to ensure the accuracy and integrity of their credit reports.

Fair Debt Collection Practices Act (FDCPA)

The Fair Debt Collection Practices Act (FDCPA) is a federal law that protects consumers from abusive, deceptive, and unfair debt collection practices. Enacted in 1977, the FDCPA applies to third-party debt collectors and covers personal, family, and household debts, including credit card debt, medical bills, and student loans. Here's what the FDCPA entails:

1. Prohibited Practices: The FDCPA prohibits debt collectors from engaging in abusive or harassing behavior, such as using threats, profanity, or calling repeatedly with the intent to annoy or harass.
2. Validation of Debts: Debt collectors are required to provide consumers with written validation of the debt within five days of initial contact. This validation must include information about the debt, the original creditor, and the consumer's rights to dispute the debt.
3. Cease and Desist: Consumers have the right to request that debt collectors cease communication with them. Once a consumer sends a written cease and desist letter, the debt collector must stop contacting them except to notify them of specific actions, such as a lawsuit.
4. False or Misleading Representations: Debt collectors are prohibited from making false or misleading statements, such as threatening legal action they cannot take or misrepresenting the amount owed.
5. Debt Collection Practices: Debt collectors are restricted in the times they can contact consumers, typically between 8:00 a.m. and 9:00 p.m. local time, and they cannot contact consumers at their workplace if they're informed that such calls are not allowed.

Understanding the FDCPA can help consumers protect themselves from abusive debt collection practices.

Consumer Financial Protection Bureau (CFPB)

The Consumer Financial Protection Bureau (CFPB) is a federal agency responsible for enforcing consumer protection laws and regulating financial institutions. Established in 2011 as part of the Dodd-Frank Wall Street Reform and Consumer Protection Act, the CFPB's mission is to protect consumers from unfair, deceptive, or abusive practices in the financial marketplace. Here's what the CFPB does:

1. Consumer Complaints: The CFPB accepts and investigates consumer complaints regarding financial products and services, including credit cards, mortgages, and student loans. Consumers can submit complaints online or by phone.
2. Rulemaking and Enforcement: The CFPB has the authority to issue rules and regulations to protect consumers and enforce compliance with existing laws. It has taken enforcement actions against financial institutions for various violations, including unfair debt collection practices and deceptive marketing.
3. Consumer Education and Outreach: The CFPB provides educational resources and tools to help consumers make informed financial decisions. This includes guides, videos, and interactive tools on topics such as budgeting, credit scores, and debt management.
4. Supervision of Financial Institutions: The CFPB supervises banks, credit unions, and other financial institutions to ensure compliance with consumer protection laws. It conducts examinations and investigations to assess compliance and address any violations.

The CFPB serves as a valuable resource for consumers seeking assistance with financial issues and complaints.

Federal Trade Commission (FTC)

The Federal Trade Commission (FTC) is a federal agency responsible for protecting consumers and promoting competition in the marketplace. Established in 1914, the FTC enforces a variety of consumer protection laws, including those related to credit and debt collection. Here's what the FTC does:

1. Enforcement of Consumer Protection Laws: The FTC enforces laws related to unfair or deceptive acts or practices, including those outlined in the FCRA and FDCPA. It investigates complaints, takes legal action against violators, and provides consumer education.
2. Consumer Education and Outreach: Similar to the CFPB, the FTC provides educational resources and materials to help consumers understand their rights and make informed decisions. This includes articles, videos, and publications on topics such as credit repair, identity theft, and scams.
3. Identity Theft Assistance: The FTC offers resources and assistance to victims of identity theft, including guidance on reporting and recovering from identity theft incidents. It operates the IdentityTheft.gov website, which provides step-by-step instructions for identity theft victims.
4. Regulation of Advertising and Marketing: The FTC regulates advertising and marketing practices to prevent deceptive or misleading advertising. This includes monitoring credit repair companies, debt relief services, and other financial services providers.

The FTC plays a critical role in protecting consumers from deceptive practices and promoting fair competition in the marketplace.

Sample Letters for Legal Remedies

When dealing with credit issues, it's essential to communicate effectively and assert your rights under the law. Below are sample letters for legal remedies under the FCRA and FDCPA:

FCRA Dispute Letter

[Your Name]
[Your Address]
[City, State, Zip Code]

[Date]

[Credit Bureau Name]
[Address]

[City, State, Zip Code]

Subject: Dispute of Inaccurate Information on Credit Report

Dear Sir/Madam,

I am writing to dispute the following information on my credit report:

- Account Name: [Name of Creditor]
- Account Number: [Account Number]
- Description of Inaccuracy: [Describe the inaccurate information, such as incorrect balance, late payment, or account status]

I believe this information is inaccurate because [Explain why you believe the information is inaccurate, providing any supporting documents or evidence].

Under the Fair Credit Reporting Act, you are required to investigate this dispute and correct any inaccuracies within 30 days. Please provide me with the results of your investigation and a corrected copy of my credit report.

Sincerely,

[Your Name]

FDCPA Cease and Desist Letter

[Your Name]
[Your Address]
[City, State, Zip Code]

[Date]

[Debt Collection Agency Name]
[Address]

[City, State, Zip Code]

Subject: Cease and Desist Communication Notice

Dear Sir/Madam,

I am writing to request that you cease all communication with me regarding the debt referenced below:

- Account Number: [Account Number]
- Amount: [Amount of Debt]

Please consider this letter as a formal request under the Fair Debt Collection Practices Act (FDCPA) to cease all communication with me, my family, and my place of employment. Any further communication should be directed to me in writing.

Sincerely,

[Your Name]

By understanding your legal rights and utilizing the resources available, you can protect yourself from unfair credit practices and take action to improve your credit. In the next chapters, we'll explore advanced strategies for credit repair and long-term financial success.

Chapter 7: Advanced Techniques

In this chapter, we'll explore advanced techniques and strategies for improving your credit score and addressing credit issues effectively. These techniques go beyond the basics and can be powerful tools in your credit repair arsenal.

Goodwill Letters

Goodwill letters are a proactive way to request a goodwill adjustment from a creditor or lender, asking them to remove negative information from your credit report. While not guaranteed to work, goodwill letters can be effective in certain situations, such as:

1. One-Time Mistakes: If you have a history of responsible credit use but experienced a one-time financial setback, such as a late payment due to illness or job loss, a goodwill letter can explain the circumstances and request leniency.
2. Customer Loyalty: If you've been a long-time customer with a creditor and have a positive relationship, they may be willing to make a goodwill adjustment as a gesture of goodwill and to retain your business.
3. Errors or Disputes: If negative information on your credit report is due to errors or inaccuracies, a goodwill letter can serve as a formal request for correction.

When writing a goodwill letter, it's essential to:

- Be polite and professional.
- Explain the circumstances honestly and concisely.
- Take responsibility for any mistakes.
- Express your commitment to maintaining good credit in the future.

Here's a sample goodwill letter template:

[Your Name]
[Your Address]
[City, State, Zip Code]

[Date]

[Name of Creditor/Lender]
[Address]

[City, State, Zip Code]

Subject: Request for Goodwill Adjustment

Dear [Creditor/Lender's Name],

I am writing to request a goodwill adjustment to my account with [Creditor/Lender]. I recently reviewed my credit report and noticed that there is a [late payment/charge-off/etc.] listed on my account from [date]. I understand that this negative information may negatively impact my credit score and future credit opportunities.

I wanted to provide some context for this late payment/charge-off/etc. [Explain the circumstances that led to the negative information, such as job loss, illness, etc.]. Despite this setback, I have maintained a positive payment history with [Creditor/Lender] for [number of years].

I am committed to maintaining good credit and would greatly appreciate it if you could consider removing this negative information from my credit report as a gesture of goodwill. Removing this information would greatly improve my credit score and help me achieve my financial goals.

Thank you for your consideration. I look forward to hearing from you soon.

Sincerely,

[Your Name]

Paying for Deletion

Paying for deletions is a negotiation strategy where you offer to pay a debt in exchange for the creditor or collection agency removing the negative information from your credit report. While not all creditors or collection agencies will agree to this arrangement, it can be an effective way to improve your credit score, especially if the negative information is significant.

When using the pay-for-deletion strategy, follow these steps:

1. Negotiate the Terms: Contact the creditor or collection agency and offer to pay the debt in full or settle for a lower amount in exchange for the removal of the negative information from your credit report.
2. Get the Agreement in Writing: If the creditor or collection agency agrees to the pay-for-deletion arrangement, make sure to get the agreement in writing before making any payments. This protects you and ensures that the terms of the agreement are clear.
3. Make the Payment: Once you have the agreement in writing, make the payment as agreed upon.
4. Follow Up: After making the payment, follow up with the creditor or collection agency to ensure that they've upheld their end of the agreement and removed the negative information from your credit report.

Here's a sample pay-for-deletion letter template:

[Your Name]
[Your Address]
[City, State, Zip Code]

[Date]

[Name of Creditor/Collection Agency]
[Address]

[City, State, Zip Code]

Subject: Pay-for-Deletion Agreement

Dear [Creditor/Collection Agency's Name],

I am writing to propose a pay-for-deletion agreement regarding the debt listed on my credit report. The debt in question is for [amount] and is listed as [describe the negative information, such as a charge-off or collection account].

I am willing to pay the full amount of the debt in exchange for the removal of this negative information from my credit report. Once the payment is received, I request that you notify all three major credit bureaus to remove this information from my credit report entirely.

Please confirm your acceptance of these terms in writing, and I will arrange for payment accordingly.

Sincerely,

[Your Name]

Rapid Resource

Rapid rescoring is a service offered by mortgage lenders to help borrowers quickly improve their credit scores in order to qualify for a mortgage or secure a better interest rate. While not available to the general public, rapid rescoring can be a valuable tool for those in the process of applying for a mortgage.

Here's how rapid rescoring works:

1. Identify Errors or Issues: The mortgage lender identifies errors or issues on the borrower's credit report that are negatively impacting their credit score. This could include outdated information, incorrect balances, or unauthorized inquiries.
2. Submit Documentation: The borrower provides documentation to support the correction of errors or issues on their credit report. This could include proof of paid-off accounts, letters of explanation for derogatory marks, or documentation of credit limits.
3. Lender Submits Request: The lender submits a rapid rescore request to the credit bureaus, along with the supporting documentation provided by the borrower.
4. Credit Bureaus Update Information: The credit bureaus review the documentation and update the borrower's credit report accordingly, typically within a few days.
5. New Credit Score: Once the credit report is updated, the borrower's credit score is recalculated based on the corrected information. This updated score is then used by the lender to determine mortgage eligibility and interest rates.

Rapid rescoring can be a valuable tool for borrowers looking to improve their credit score quickly in order to qualify for a mortgage or secure a better interest rate.

Authorized User Strategy

The authorized user strategy involves becoming an authorized user on someone else's credit card account to benefit from their positive credit history. This can be a family member, spouse, or friend who has a well-established credit history and responsible credit behavior.

Here's how the authorized user strategy works:

1. Find a Trusted Partner: Identify someone with a good credit history who is willing to add you as an authorized user on their credit card account. It's essential to choose someone who is responsible with their credit and has a long history of on-time payments.
2. Become an Authorized User: Once you've identified a trusted partner, they can add you as an authorized user on their credit card account. You'll receive a credit card with your name on it, but the primary account holder remains responsible for the account.
3. Benefit from Positive History: As an authorized user, you'll benefit from the primary account holder's positive credit history. This can include their on-time payments, low credit utilization, and long credit history, all of which can positively impact your credit score.
4. Monitor Your Credit: Keep track of your credit report and score to ensure that the account is being reported accurately and positively impacting your credit. If there are any issues, you can address them with the credit bureaus.

While the authorized user strategy can be an effective way to improve your credit score, it's essential to choose a trusted partner and monitor your credit to ensure that the arrangement is benefiting you positively.

Disputing Certified Mail

Disputing inaccuracies on your credit report via certified mail is a method to ensure that your dispute is received and processed by the credit bureaus. When disputing errors on your credit report, it's essential to do so in writing and to send your dispute via certified mail to have a record of delivery.

Here's how to dispute inaccuracies via certified mail:

1. Write a Dispute Letter: Draft a dispute letter detailing the inaccuracies on your credit report, including any supporting documentation. Be clear and concise in your explanation of the errors and what you're requesting from the credit bureaus.
2. Send via Certified Mail: Print and sign your dispute letter, then send it via certified mail with the return receipt requested. This ensures that you have proof of delivery and that the credit bureaus received your dispute.
3. Keep Records: Keep a copy of your dispute letter, along with the certified mail receipt and any other documentation related to your dispute. This serves as evidence in case you need to escalate your dispute further.
4. Follow-up: After sending your dispute, allow the credit bureaus 30 days to investigate and respond. If you don't receive a response within that time frame or if the inaccuracies are not corrected, follow up with the credit bureaus and provide additional evidence if necessary.

Here's a sample dispute letter template:

[Your Name]
[Your Address]
[City, State, Zip Code]

[Date]

[Credit Bureau Name]
[Address]

[City, State, Zip Code]

Subject: Dispute of Inaccurate Information on Credit Report

Dear Sir/Madam,

I am writing to dispute the following information on my credit report:

- Account Name: [Name of Creditor]
- Account Number: [Account Number]
- Description of Inaccuracy: [Describe the inaccurate information, such as incorrect balance, late payment, or account status]

I believe this information is inaccurate because [Explain why you believe the information is inaccurate, providing any supporting documents or evidence].

Under the Fair Credit Reporting Act, you are required to investigate this dispute and correct any inaccuracies within 30 days. Please provide me with the results of your investigation and a corrected copy of my credit report.

Sincerely,

[Your Name]

Disputing inaccuracies via certified mail ensures that your dispute is received and processed by the credit bureaus, giving you a better chance of having the errors corrected.

By utilizing these advanced techniques and strategies, you can take proactive steps to improve your credit score and address credit issues effectively. In the next chapters, we'll explore long-term maintenance strategies and tips for achieving financial stability.

Chapter 8: Long-Term Maintenance

Maintaining good credit isn't just about fixing past mistakes; it's also about establishing healthy financial habits that will serve you well in the long run. In this chapter, we'll delve into the importance of regular monitoring, avoiding credit repair scams, staying financially responsible, and planning for the future.

Importance of Regular Monitoring

Regularly monitoring your credit is like keeping tabs on your financial health. Just as you would monitor your physical health with regular check-ups, monitoring your credit helps you catch any issues early and take action to address them. Here's why it's crucial:

1. Early Detection of Errors: Mistakes happen, and your credit report is no exception. By checking your credit report regularly, you can spot errors such as inaccuracies in your personal information, accounts that don't belong to you, or fraudulent activity.
2. Preventing Identity Theft: Identity theft is a prevalent concern in today's digital age. Regularly monitoring your credit report allows you to detect any signs of identity theft, such as unauthorized accounts or inquiries, and take steps to mitigate the damage.
3. Maintaining Good Credit Health: Monitoring your credit helps you keep track of your credit score and understand how your financial decisions impact it. You can see the effects of paying bills on time, reducing credit card balances, and managing debt responsibly.
4. Preparing for Major Financial Decisions: Whether you're applying for a mortgage, car loan, or new credit card, having a good credit score is essential. Regular monitoring allows you to identify areas for improvement and take action to boost your score before applying for credit.

To monitor your credit effectively:

- Check Your Credit Report Regularly: Federal law entitles you to one free credit report from each of the three major credit bureaus (Equifax, Experian, and TransUnion) every 12 months through AnnualCreditReport.com. Take advantage of this and review your report for any errors or suspicious activity.
- Sign Up for Credit Monitoring Services: Many credit card issuers and financial institutions offer free credit monitoring services that provide regular updates on changes to your credit report. Consider enrolling in such services to receive alerts about important changes.
- Set Reminders: Make it a habit to check your credit report regularly, whether it's once a month, quarterly, or annually. Set reminders on your calendar or use mobile apps to help you remember.

Regular monitoring empowers you to take control of your financial well-being and protect yourself from potential threats to your credit.

Avoiding Credit Repair Scams

While there are legitimate credit repair services that can help you navigate the process of improving your credit, there are also many scams out there that prey on individuals seeking quick fixes. It's essential to be aware of the warning signs of credit repair scams and know how to protect yourself:

1. Promises of Guaranteed Results: Be wary of credit repair companies that guarantee they can remove negative information from your credit report or improve your credit score. Legitimate credit repair takes time and effort, and there are no guarantees of specific outcomes.
2. Upfront Fees: The Credit Repair Organizations Act (CROA) prohibits credit repair companies from charging upfront fees for their services. If a company asks for payment before performing any work, it's a red flag.
3. Pressure Tactics: Avoid companies that use high-pressure sales tactics or make you feel uncomfortable. Legitimate credit repair companies should be transparent about their services and fees and should never pressure you into signing up.
4. Lack of Transparency: Legitimate credit repair companies should provide clear information about their services, including how they'll help you, how long it will take, and how much it will cost. If a company is vague or unwilling to answer your questions, steer clear.
5. Unwillingness to Provide Written Agreements: Legitimate credit repair companies should provide you with a written contract outlining the terms and conditions of their services. If a company is unwilling to provide a written agreement, it's a sign that it may not be legitimate.

To protect yourself from credit repair scams:

- Research Companies Thoroughly: Before hiring a credit repair company, research them thoroughly. Check their reputation with the Better Business Bureau, read reviews from other customers, and look for any complaints or legal actions against them.
- Understand Your Rights: Familiarize yourself with the Credit Repair Organizations Act (CROA) and your rights as a consumer. Knowing what credit repair companies can and cannot do will help you spot scams more easily.
- Trust Your Instincts: If something seems too good to be true or you feel uncomfortable with a company, trust your instincts and walk away.

By staying vigilant and informed, you can avoid falling victim to credit repair scams and focus on legitimate ways to improve your credit.

Staying Financially Responsible

Maintaining good credit isn't just about fixing past mistakes; it's also about adopting healthy financial habits that promote long-term financial stability. Here are some key practices to help you stay financially responsible:

1. Pay Bills on Time: Your payment history accounts for a significant portion of your credit score, so paying bills on time is crucial. Set up automatic payments or reminders to ensure you never miss a due date.
2. Keep Credit Card Balances Low: High credit card balances can negatively impact your credit utilization ratio, which is the amount of credit you're using compared to your total available credit. Aim to keep your balances below 30% of your credit limit.
3. Avoid Opening Too Many Accounts: Opening multiple new credit accounts within a short period can indicate financial instability and lower your credit score. Only apply for new credit when necessary and avoid unnecessary inquiries.
4. Monitor Your Credit Regularly: As discussed earlier, regular monitoring of your credit report helps you stay informed about changes to your credit and detect any errors or suspicious activity early.
5. Build an Emergency Fund: Having an emergency fund can help you avoid relying on credit cards or loans in times of financial need. Aim to save at least three to six months' worth of living expenses in an easily accessible account.
6. Create and Stick to a Budget: A budget helps you track your income and expenses and ensures that you're living within your means. Identify areas where you can cut back on spending and prioritize saving and debt repayment.
7. Educate Yourself: Take the time to educate yourself about personal finance topics such as budgeting, investing, and credit management. The more you know, the better equipped you'll be to make informed financial decisions.

By adopting these financial habits and making them a part of your daily routine, you can maintain good credit and achieve long-term financial success.

Future Planning

Planning for the future is an essential aspect of maintaining good credit and overall financial well-being. Whether you're saving for retirement, buying a home, or starting a family, having a solid financial plan in place can help you achieve your goals. Here are some key areas to consider when planning for the future:

1. Retirement Savings: Start saving for retirement as early as possible to take advantage of compound interest and maximize your savings. Contribute to employer-sponsored retirement plans such as 401(k)s or open an individual retirement account (IRA).
2. Emergency Fund: As mentioned earlier, having an emergency fund is crucial for financial stability. Aim to save enough to cover three to six months' worth of living expenses in case of unexpected events such as job loss or medical emergencies.
3. Homeownership: If homeownership is a goal, start saving for a down payment and work on improving your credit score to qualify for a mortgage with favorable terms. Consider factors such as location, housing affordability, and long-term financial commitment.
4. Education Savings: If you have children or plan to pursue further education yourself, start saving for education expenses early. Consider options such as 529 college savings plans or education savings accounts (ESAs).
5. Estate Planning: Plan for the distribution of your assets and the care of your loved ones in the event of your incapacity or death. Create a will, establish powers of attorney, and consider setting up trusts to protect your assets and minimize taxes.
6. Insurance Coverage: Review your insurance coverage regularly to ensure that you have adequate protection for your home, vehicles, health, and life. Consider factors such as coverage limits, deductibles, and premiums.
7. Investment Strategy: Develop an investment strategy that aligns with your financial goals, risk tolerance, and time horizon. Consider diversifying your investments across different asset classes to manage risk effectively.

By planning for the future and taking proactive steps to achieve your financial goals, you can create a solid foundation for long-term financial success and maintain good credit along the way.

In conclusion, maintaining good credit requires a combination of vigilance, responsible financial habits, and forward-thinking planning. By regularly monitoring your credit, avoiding scams, staying financially responsible, and planning for the future, you can build and maintain a healthy credit profile that serves you well throughout your life. In the next chapter, we'll summarize key takeaways and provide a roadmap for putting these principles into action.

Chapter 9: Case Studies and Success Stories

In this chapter, we'll explore real-life examples of individuals who successfully repaired their credit. These case studies provide valuable insights into the credit repair process, lessons learned along the way, and inspiration for readers facing similar challenges.

Real Life Examples of Credit Repair

Case Study 1: John's Journey to Credit Recovery

John, a recent college graduate, found himself in a financial predicament after accumulating credit card debt and missing payments while juggling student loans and living expenses. His credit score plummeted, making it difficult for him to qualify for a car loan or rent an apartment.

Initial Situation: John's credit score was in the low 500s, primarily due to missed payments and high credit card balances.

Credit Repair Strategy: John took a proactive approach to repairing his credit by:

1. Creating a Budget: He created a detailed budget to track his income and expenses, allowing him to prioritize debt repayment and avoid overspending.
2. Negotiating with Creditors: John contacted his creditors to negotiate lower interest rates and payment plans. Some creditors agreed to settle for less than the full amount owed, helping him pay off debts faster.
3. Disputing Inaccuracies: He carefully reviewed his credit reports and disputed any inaccuracies or errors. By providing documentation and following up with the credit bureaus, he was able to remove negative items from his report.
4. Building Positive Credit History: John applied for a secured credit card and used it responsibly, making small purchases and paying the balance in full each month. This helped him establish a positive payment history and improve his credit utilization ratio.

Results: Over the course of two years, John's credit score gradually increased from the low 500s to the mid-600s. He was able to qualify for a car loan at a reasonable interest rate and secure an apartment lease without a cosigner.

Case Study 2: Sarah's Struggle with Identity Theft

Sarah, a working professional in her thirties, discovered that she was a victim of identity theft when she received a collection notice for a credit card she never opened. The fraudulent account had damaged her credit score and left her feeling overwhelmed and frustrated.

Initial Situation: Sarah's credit score had dropped significantly due to fraudulent accounts and unauthorized inquiries.

Credit Repair Strategy: Sarah took swift action to address the identity theft and repair her credit by:

1. Reporting Identity Theft: She filed a police report and submitted a fraud alert to the credit bureaus, notifying them of the fraudulent activity on her credit report.
2. Freezing Credit Reports: Sarah placed a freeze on her credit reports to prevent further unauthorized accounts from being opened in her name.
3. Disputing Fraudulent Accounts: She disputed the fraudulent accounts and inquiries with the credit bureaus, providing evidence of the identity theft.
4. Monitoring Credit Regularly: Sarah signed up for credit monitoring services to keep track of changes to her credit report and receive alerts about suspicious activity.

Results: Despite the initial setback, Sarah's credit score gradually improved as the fraudulent accounts were removed from her credit report. She was able to rebuild her credit and regain financial stability within a year.

Lessons Learned

1. Take Immediate Action: Both John and Sarah took immediate action to address their credit issues, whether it was negotiating with creditors, disputing inaccuracies, or reporting identity theft. Taking action sooner rather than later is key to minimizing the impact on your credit score.
2. Persistence Pays Off: Repairing credit takes time and persistence. John and Sarah didn't give up, even when faced with challenges along the way. By staying focused on their goals and taking proactive steps, they were able to achieve success.
3. Educate Yourself: Understanding how credit works and your rights as a consumer is crucial when repairing credit. John and Sarah educated themselves about credit repair strategies, consumer protection laws, and how to navigate the credit system effectively.
4. Be Patient: Rebuilding credit is a gradual process. John and Sarah didn't expect overnight results but remained patient and committed to their goals. Over time, their efforts paid off, and they saw significant improvements in their credit scores.
5. Monitor Your Credit: Regularly monitoring your credit is essential for detecting errors, inaccuracies, or signs of fraud early. John and Sarah made monitoring their credit a priority, allowing them to address issues promptly and prevent further damage to their credit.

Inspiration for Readers

The stories of John and Sarah serve as inspiration for readers facing similar credit challenges. Despite facing financial setbacks and obstacles, they were able to overcome them and achieve success. Their stories demonstrate that with determination, persistence, and the right strategies, it's possible to repair credit and regain financial stability.

If you're struggling with credit issues, remember:

- You're not alone. Many people face challenges with credit at some point in their lives.
- It's never too late to start repairing your credit. Regardless of your current situation, there are steps you can take to improve your credit score.
- Small changes can make a big difference. Whether it's paying bills on time, reducing credit card balances, or disputing inaccuracies, every positive action counts.
- Stay focused on your goals and be patient. Credit repair takes time, but with consistent effort, you can achieve the results you're aiming for.

By learning from the experiences of others and taking proactive steps to improve your credit, you can create a brighter financial future for yourself. Remember, the journey to better credit begins with the first step.

Chapter 10: Additional Resources

In this chapter, we'll provide you with valuable resources to support your journey toward repairing and maintaining good credit. From contact information for credit bureaus and consumer agencies to recommended books, websites, and a glossary of terms, these resources will equip you with the tools and knowledge you need to succeed.

Contact Information for Credit Bureaus

Credit bureaus play a vital role in the credit reporting system by collecting and maintaining information about your credit history. Here's the contact information for the three major credit bureaus in the United States:

1. Equifax
    - Website: www.equifax.com
    - Phone: 1-866-349-5191
    - Address: Equifax Information Services LLC, P.O. Box 740256, Atlanta, GA 30374
2. Experian
    - Website: www.experian.com
    - Phone: 1-888-397-3742
    - Address: Experian, P.O. Box 4500, Allen, TX 75013
3. TransUnion
    - Website: www.transunion.com
    - Phone: 1-800-916-8800
    - Address: TransUnion LLC, P.O. Box 2000, Chester, PA 19016

When contacting the credit bureaus, be prepared to provide your personal information, such as your full name, address, date of birth, and Social Security number, to verify your identity.

Contact Information for Consumer Agencies

Consumer agencies provide valuable resources and assistance to consumers dealing with credit issues, identity theft, and other financial concerns. Here are some key consumer agencies and their contact information:

1. Consumer Financial Protection Bureau (CFPB)
    - Website: www.consumerfinance.gov
    - Phone: 1-855-411-2372
    - Address: Consumer Financial Protection Bureau, P.O. Box 4503, Iowa City, Iowa 52244
2. Federal Trade Commission (FTC)
    - Website: www.ftc.gov
    - Phone: 1-877-FTC-HELP (1-877-382-4357)
    - Address: Federal Trade Commission, Consumer Response Center, 600 Pennsylvania Avenue, NW, Washington, DC 20580
3. IdentityTheft.gov
    - Website: www.identitytheft.gov
    - Phone: 1-877-ID-THEFT (1-877-438-4338)
    - Address: Federal Trade Commission, Identity Theft Clearinghouse, 600 Pennsylvania Avenue, NW, Washington, DC 20580

These agencies offer a wealth of information, resources, and assistance to help you navigate credit-related issues and protect yourself from fraud and scams.

Recommended Books and Websites

1. Books
    - *Credit Repair Kit For Dummies* by Steve Bucci: This comprehensive guide covers everything you need to know about repairing your credit, from understanding credit reports to disputing inaccuracies and rebuilding credit.
    - *The Total Money Makeover* by Dave Ramsey: While not solely focused on credit repair, this book provides practical advice for getting out of debt, building wealth, and achieving financial freedom.
    - *Your Score: An Insider's Secrets to Understanding, Controlling, and Protecting Your Credit Score* by Anthony Davenport: This book offers insider tips and strategies for understanding and improving your credit score.
2. Websites
    - Credit Karma (www.creditkarma.com): Credit Karma offers free access to your credit scores and reports from Equifax and TransUnion. It also provides personalized recommendations for improving your credit.
    - AnnualCreditReport.com: This website allows you to request a free copy of your credit report from each of the three major credit bureaus once every 12 months.
    - MyFICO (www.myfico.com): MyFICO provides access to your FICO credit scores and offers tools and resources for understanding and managing your credit.

Glossary of Terms

To help you navigate the complex world of credit, here's a glossary of common terms you'll encounter:

1. Credit Score: A numerical representation of your creditworthiness, based on factors such as payment history, credit utilization, and length of credit history.
2. Credit Report: A detailed record of your credit history, including accounts, payment history, inquiries, and public records.
3. Credit Bureau: A company that collects and maintains information about consumers' credit history and provides credit reports to lenders.
4. Credit Utilization Ratio: The ratio of your credit card balances to your credit limits, expressed as a percentage. A lower ratio is generally better for your credit score.
5. Credit Inquiry: A record of when someone requests to view your credit report, typically as part of a credit application process.
6. Dispute: A process for challenging inaccuracies or errors on your credit report with the credit bureaus.
7. Identity Theft: The unauthorized use of someone else's personal information to commit fraud or other crimes.
8. Secured Credit Card: A credit card that requires a security deposit as collateral, typically used by individuals with limited or poor credit history.
9. Unsecured Credit: Credit that is not backed by collateral, such as credit cards or personal loans.
10. Debt Settlement: Negotiating with creditors to settle a debt for less than the full amount owed, typically as a lump-sum payment.
11. Bankruptcy: A legal process for individuals or businesses to seek relief from debts they cannot repay, typically resulting in the discharge of debts or a repayment plan.
12. Credit Counseling: Professional counseling services that help individuals manage debt and improve their financial situation.
13. Credit Freeze: A security measure that restricts access to your credit report, making it more difficult for identity thieves to open new accounts in your name.
14. Goodwill Letter: A letter sent to a creditor or lender requesting the removal of negative information from your credit report as a gesture of goodwill.
15. Pay-for-Delete: A negotiation strategy where you offer to pay a debt in exchange for the creditor or collection agency removing the negative information from your credit report.

This glossary provides a basic understanding of key credit terms and concepts, helping you navigate the credit repair process with confidence.

By utilizing these additional resources, you can enhance your understanding of credit, access valuable tools and information, and take proactive steps toward improving and maintaining your credit health. Whether you're disputing inaccuracies on your credit report, seeking financial guidance, or educating yourself about credit management, these resources are here to support you on your journey to financial success.

Conclusion

As you reach the end of this guide, you've embarked on a journey towards repairing and maintaining your credit. We've covered a range of topics, from understanding credit reports and scores to disputing inaccuracies, rebuilding credit, and adopting healthy financial habits. Now, let's recap the key points and offer encouragement for the future.

Recap of Points

1. Understanding Credit Reports and Scores: Your credit report is a detailed record of your credit history, while your credit score is a numerical representation of your creditworthiness. It's essential to review your credit reports regularly, understand the factors that influence your credit score, and monitor changes over time.
2. Disputing Inaccuracies: If you find errors or inaccuracies on your credit report, you have the right to dispute them with the credit bureaus. This involves submitting a formal dispute letter and providing supporting documentation to back up your claims.
3. Strategies for Improving Credit: There are several strategies you can use to improve your credit, including paying down debt, negotiating with creditors, using secured credit cards, and building a positive credit history. By adopting these strategies and staying financially responsible, you can gradually raise your credit score.
4. Dealing with Collections: If you have accounts in collections, you can negotiate settlements or pay-for-delete agreements to resolve them. It's essential to communicate with collection agencies and work towards finding a solution that works for both parties.
5. Rebuilding Credit: Rebuilding credit takes time and patience. You can start by applying for new credit, improving credit utilization, using credit builder loans, and monitoring your progress regularly.
6. Legal Rights and Resources: Understanding your rights under the Fair Credit Reporting Act (FCRA) and the Fair Debt Collection Practices Act (FDCPA) empowers you to take action against inaccurate information or abusive debt collection practices. Consumer agencies like the Consumer Financial Protection Bureau (CFPB) and the Federal Trade Commission (FTC) offer valuable resources and assistance.
7. Advanced Techniques: Goodwill letters, paying for deletions, rapid rescore, authorized user strategy, and disputing via certified mail are advanced techniques you can use to address specific credit issues and improve your score.
8. Long-Term Maintenance: Regular monitoring of your credit, avoiding credit repair scams, staying financially responsible, and planning for the future are essential for maintaining good credit in the long term.
9. Case Studies and Success Stories: Real-life examples demonstrate that with determination, persistence, and the right strategies, it's possible to repair credit and achieve financial stability.
10. Additional Resources: Contact information for credit bureaus, consumer agencies, recommended books, websites, and a glossary of terms provide valuable tools and information to support your credit repair journey.

Encouragement for the Future

Repairing and maintaining good credit is a journey, not a destination. It requires dedication, patience, and a willingness to learn and adapt. As you continue on your path, here are some words of encouragement for the future:

1. Stay Committed: Building good credit takes time and effort. Stay committed to your goals, and don't get discouraged by setbacks along the way. Every positive step you take brings you closer to financial freedom.
2. Educate Yourself: Knowledge is power when it comes to credit. Take the time to educate yourself about credit management, consumer rights, and financial literacy. The more you know, the better equipped you'll be to make informed decisions.
3. Celebrate Progress: Celebrate your achievements, no matter how small. Whether it's paying off a credit card, improving your credit score, or reaching a financial milestone, acknowledge your progress and use it as motivation to keep moving forward.
4. Seek Support: Don't be afraid to seek support from friends, family, or financial professionals. Surround yourself with people who encourage and support your efforts to improve your credit and achieve your financial goals.
5. Stay Positive: Maintaining a positive attitude can make all the difference. Even when faced with challenges or setbacks, approach them with optimism and a belief in your ability to overcome them.
6. Set Realistic Goals: Set realistic, achievable goals for yourself and create a plan to reach them. Whether it's paying off debt, increasing your credit score, or saving for a major purchase, break your goals down into smaller, manageable steps.
7. Keep Learning and Growing: The world of credit and finance is constantly evolving. Stay informed about changes in the industry, new laws and regulations, and emerging trends. Continuously seek opportunities to learn and grow.
8. Pay It Forward: Once you've successfully repaired your credit, consider paying it forward by sharing your knowledge and experience with others. You never know how your story might inspire someone else to take control of their financial future.

As you move forward on your credit repair journey, remember that you have the power to shape your financial destiny. By taking control of your credit, making smart financial decisions, and staying focused on your goals, you can build a brighter and more secure future for yourself and your loved ones.

Best of luck on your journey, and may your future be filled with financial success and prosperity.

Other Books By This Publisher

Good Sense Publishing https://amzn.to/3yrTJal

Other Books By This Author

DIY Divorce in South Carolina https://amzn.to/4dP48x2

Notary Journal https://amzn.to/4bBLQgO

About This Author

Oliver Firestone is a best-selling author renowned for his practical and insightful guides that help individuals navigate complex personal and financial challenges. Born and raised in Atlanta, Georgia, Oliver's Southern roots have greatly influenced his approach to writing—infusing his work with warmth, wit, and a deep understanding of the regional nuances that affect his readers.

Currently residing in South Carolina, Oliver has become a go-to resource for people seeking straightforward advice on intricate issues. His breakout success came with the publication of "DIY Guide to Divorce in South Carolina," a comprehensive manual that demystifies the divorce process in the state, offering clear, actionable steps for those going through this difficult life transition.

In addition to his guide on divorce, Oliver has authored several specialized journals for notaries, providing invaluable resources that aid these professionals in maintaining meticulous records and upholding high standards of practice. His knack for transforming complicated legal and procedural content into accessible and user-friendly material has earned him a dedicated following.

Oliver's most recent work, "Fix Your F ing, I Mean Failing, Credit," showcases his ability to tackle financial recovery with both candor and humor. This book addresses the often daunting task of credit repair, offering readers practical strategies to improve their financial health and regain control over their economic futures.

When not writing, Oliver retreats to his mountain hideaway in North Carolina. It is in this tranquil setting that he finds the inspiration and focus needed to craft his next bestseller. This peaceful retreat allows him to escape the hustle and bustle, providing a perfect backdrop for his creative process.

Oliver Firestone continues to empower his readers with the knowledge and tools they need to navigate life's legal and financial hurdles, making him a beloved and influential voice in the world of self-help and practical guides.

Review This Book

P.S. It Means the world to me that you bought my book. Writing is my passion and I look forward to YOUR feedback.

So if you liked this book, I'd like to ask for a small favor. Would you be so kind to leave a review on Amazon? It'd be very much appreciated!

From your friend,
Oliver Firestone

Leave A Review
https://www.amazon.com/review/create-review/?ie=UTF8&channel=glance-detail&asin=B0D4NNFF9D

This book is intended for entertainment purposes only and does not constitute legal advice. While the information provided aims to be accurate and helpful, it should not be relied upon as a substitute for professional legal counsel. Readers are encouraged to consult with a qualified attorney for advice on specific legal matters. The author and publisher disclaim any liability for any actions taken based on the information contained in this book.

www.ingramcontent.com/pod-product-compliance
Lightning Source LLC
Chambersburg PA
CBHW082357220526
45470CB00008B/2779